Here's what people are saying about NAKED . . .

"Founding member of the seminal spoken-word initiative the Last Poets, thought by many critics to be the first hip hop group, Oyewole is a sublime force of scholarship and creativity. A born storyteller, he has infused his newest collection with a powerful sense of humanity. With an exuberant and informative introduction by Lyah Beth LeFlore, *NAKED* is a solid and universal volume by a masterful poet." **~Raúl Niño, *Booklist***

"In *NAKED,* Abiodun Oyewole bares the soul of an older, wiser, somewhat vulnerable, yet ever eloquent warrior-poet. Still standing strong, in this collection of poems he artfully calls upon nature, our history and our inner strength to remind us of our resilience, our purpose and our beauty. Once again he shows us the way. If I were still an English teacher this would be required reading!" **~Marcia Lyles, Retired Superintendent, Jersey City Public Schools, Former Deputy Chancellor for Teaching and Learning, NYCDOE**

"Abiodun Oyewole has no comparison because he is the source material: your favorite old school rapper's favorite old school rapper. Without The Last Poets, there may have been no Hip-Hop, and without Oyewole, there may have been no Last Poets. When a living legend gives us a gift, we have only one answer—thank you." **~Aaron Samuels, Co-Founder of Blavity Inc., author of *Yarmulkes & Fitted Caps* (2013)**

"Beyond the craft and musicality of *NAKED,* the book itself gives me great joy. To once again sit in my deep and abundant gratitude for the work and legacy of Abiodun Oyewole, who has shown so many of us the ways that language can stretch. The way images can breathe on the page. All of that is still here, in

this work. An honor to be in praise of this brilliant poet, who lit a path for so many, and who continues to do so in this book."
~**Hanif Abdurraqib, poet, essayist, cultural critic and the author of *Go Ahead in the Rain: Notes to a A Tribe Called Quest* (2019) and *A Fortune For Your Disaster* (2019)**

"Abiodun Oyewole embarks on a walk through time and space in *NAKED,* revealing the ponderings of a man looking back at time—refusing to yield. These poems lie bare like leaves in a park taking the rain of life, its heat, and the cold, but remain fresh as if only just falling to the grass." ~**Jason N. Vasser-Elong, poet, professor and the author of *shrimp* (2018)**

"Abiodun Oyewole's *NAKED* explores being exposed as Black endurance and survival. The Last Poets statesman looks at his own vulnerabilities, but also praises and loves those who avoid flinching. *NAKED* reminds us that we are like trees with cycles of flourishing and gathering strength in bare branches." ~**Tara Betts, poet, professor and the author of *Break the Habit: Poems* (2016)**

NAKED

ABIODUN OYEWOLE

A NEW POETRY COLLECTION

Introduction by Lyah Beth Leflore

FLORIDA | NEW YORK
www.2leafpress.org

P.O. Box 4378
Grand Central Station
New York, New York 10163-4378
editor@2leafpress.org
www.2leafpress.org

2LEAF PRESS INC. is a
nonprofit 501(c)(3) organization that promotes
multicultural literature and literacy.
www.2lpinc.org

Book design and layout: Gabrielle David

Library of Congress Control Number: 2020932722

ISBN-13: 978-1-7346181-0-5 (Paperback)
ISBN-13: 978-1-7346181-3-6 (eBook)

10   9   8   7   6   5   4   3   2   1

Published in the United States of America

2Leaf Press trade distribution is handled by University of Chicago Press / Chicago Distribution Center (www.press.uchicago.edu) 773.702.7010. Titles are also available for corporate, premium, and special sales. Please direct inquiries to the UCP Sales Department, 773.702.7248.

This collection of poetry is dedicated to Ace (Judy); my mother who still gives me great advice; to my brothers Rahim and Cornell; to my sisters Anita and Janice; to my children Pharoah, Aina, Oba, Ebon, Ade, Donjiman and Sowande; to Masani (a great poet and friend); and to all the trees I talk to and mother nature herself. She provides me with the very essence of what poetry is, and to all of my friends who have felt the way I feel about the nakedness of life. Finally to my publisher Gabrielle who has given me a platform to share my work with the world in a way I could have never imagined.

Nakedness has no color: this can come as news only to those who have never covered, or been covered by, another naked human being.

~James Baldwin

POEMS

INTRODUCTION

by Lyah Beth LeFlore

PERHAPS THE MOST PROFOUND moment of one's life is when you find yourself standing in front of the bathroom mirror, in all your glory, dripping wet. Wiping the steam away, an uncomfortable image comes into focus. It is YOU. As you stare into the eyes of yourself, with intrigue, and a bit of suspicion, you suddenly find yourself *unrecognizable.* The stranger peers back, equally inquisitive. There is no place to hide. Every bump, ripple, blemish, scar, and secret, on grand display. No Covergirl or high-end concealer from Sephora to camouflage, and help you blend into the stark white walls. There is no lie you can tell yourself. It is the truth of it all. You are exposed in the most vulnerable, surrendered space. You are NAKED.

The proverbial mask has been removed, much like what Paul Laurence Dunbar's poem, "We Wear The Masks," speaks of. Metaphorically, the "masks" are a sobering and searing reminder of the societal ills, we as black folk have internalized, and carried for generations. Forced to hide our pain, true selves and feelings, we have gotten used to the living the façade, frontin' and stuntin'. We have forgotten who we are.

I pondered the title of this book for days after receiving it. I delved into the very etymology of it, peeled back its meaning, and in its simplistic state, seeing much of my late mother, St. Louis Poet Laureate Emeritus, Shirley Bradley Price LeFlore's, life. Hers, like the poems that reside in this book embody, was one that was both complex and complicated, uninhibited and unapologetic, wild yet quiet, even a bit messy at times, like my own as I stand here half a century in.

I let loose a maniacal laugh inside. I'll be damned! Abiodun Oyewole has struck gold with one small word that carries such a deep and layered meaning. Poem after poem, I find myself in search of scripture. I grab my grandmother's old Bible, flip to the story of Job to be exact. See Job was a righteous and upright man, wealthy, with cattle and land, but Satan tests him and Job is suddenly stripped of everything.

In his suffering and mourning, he hits rock bottom, yet, he never waivers professing his faith and trust in God: *Then Job stood up, tore his robe, and shaved his head. He fell to the ground and worshiped, saying: "Naked I came from my mother's womb, and naked I shall return. The LORD gave, and the LORD has taken away."* Job was restored.

So, as I turn back to the healing balm cradled in the bosom of these poems, at this most perilous time of sheltering in place, masking up, and social distancing, the words strangely parallel that scripture. One doesn't have to be deeply religious or spiritual to see that in our naked selves, WE/US/I are/am a modern day Job.

Like Job, as the world quarantined, this time of stillness, introspection, and reflection shines a light on who we are as men, women, and those who would rather be recognized as "others."

WE/US/I are/am...NAKED...

We have found ourselves depleted, our cups done ran over and are dry. Our circuits burned out, worn out, weary, and broken. But Abiodun has found the anecdote, the serum, the good shit to help us press reset, re-collect, and rebuild. He writes:

I am strong
That's why I'm still standing
The wind doesn't bother me
The rain refreshes
I am washed clean with love drops from heaven
I have nothing to hide

And just like that tree he metaphorically speaks of, planted solidly in the ground; I know my own roots run deep and are impenetrable. They lead to roads that my ancestors paved. From its branches hang the stories my mother passed on about her mother, and her mother's mother, and mother before that. Harriet

Casey was a slave, and my great-great-grandfather, a free man purchased her freedom. I am one of the many fruits it bore. It is a tree that has experienced the great metamorphosis that Abiodun tells so vividly.

Yet, this tree, too, has been barren at times, parts rotted out from drought. Then those old parts die and break off, crumble, wither, dissolve into the soil, or blow away with the wind. From winter's freeze, to summer's scorch; eventually, the raging winds came, and the rain followed, feeding its thirsty roots. A new day rises, and the sun returns. The tree is still standing firm, sure-footed, and washed clean again.

The journey in *NAKED*, is a testament to all of our lives. In this crucial and necessary downtime, its words encourage us. We know even in the darkest hours, we must hold on to hope, our dreams, and a mustard seed of faith. Abiodun says:

Then faith smiles at me
Gives me more fuel to fight

Yaaaasss, Lawd! People, prepare for GOD'S CALL, because WE BE NAKED, and in need of a MOMENT OF PRAYER. And as SALVATION brings this lyrical revelation to a close, you have joined me. We have walked through the fire with his words, and Abiodun's poems have doused our burning flames within.

Can you feel it? *NAKED* is rhythmic, soulful, off beat, yet in time, and on time. Abiodun's words echo:

We must save ourselves
Or live and die in hell

Stop the fires from raging
Be more engaging
Let love be our light

The poetry up in here is a universal thang, ya'll. No barriers. It don't discriminate against age, color, religion, or sexual orientation. This is that real deal "Hollyfied." Like the old folk in St. Louis used to say, "he be kickin' the Willy Bobo!" Then saint *and* the sinner. The rich *and* the poor. 'Cause we all bleed, laugh, cry, tremble, die, and dream. *NAKED* is for public consumption. Its purpose is to nourish our emotional lives, and broaden our world view; to push beyond the boundaries and confines of your mind's eye, as it re-frames us, re-trains us, and re-leases us.

This beautiful and soulful journey has brought me full circle with myself. I am the image in the mirror. Once lost, but now found! No longer unrecognizable, drenched, skin as fresh as morning dew, purged. The Good Reverend Doctor Abiodun Oyewole's words are searing and lyrical, pure and uncut, like one of those deep Southern sanctified sermons. *NAKED!* ◉

Facts which at first seem improbable
will, even on scant explanation, drop
the cloak which has hidden them and
stand forth in naked and simple beauty.

~Galileo Galilei

On Being Here

I came from Cincinnati
With guns blazing at three
Decided on who my parents would be
Very early I designed the life
I wanted to see
With music in my heart
And poetry on my tongue
I carved out my place on the planet
While I was still young
Love was always my foundation
Life was always an education
A father from Georgia
Who believed you should work to live
A mother who said I was special
And I had so much to give
I was loved and adored
And encouraged to use my gifts
And with mother as a coach
I gave myself and others a lift

I know my life has been a blessing
And a wealth that money can't buy
I still try hard to learn all the lessons
And be someone who I can always rely.

Naked

The tree was naked
No leaves
No bark
Standing there
In the middle
Of lush trees
Fully dressed in green
Some even wore red
This tree caught my eye
I could even hear it say
You've been looking
All around me
You don't see me
Because I'm naked
I reveal my shape
My unclothed body
To the world
I am strong

That's why I'm still standing
The wind doesn't bother me
The rain refreshes me
I am washed clean
With love drops from heaven
I have nothing to hide.

Autumn

She undresses
Right in front of me
I watch her as she strips
Standing there with nothing on
Her body is bare
For everyone to see
I admire her shape
The curves and the muscles
She protected me all summer
Held me close
Sheltered me
From the tongue of the sun
Trying to lick me to death
Sometimes when she undresses
She changes the colors of her garments
From green to red
To orange to yellow to brown
Showing off her wardrobe
But now she has disrobed

Wearing nothing at all
Feeling the cool breeze blowing
Against her exposed skin
Brazen and bold she stands
Amused by those who dress up.

Older But Not Old

We are all getting older
But you don't have to get old
The years take us through changes
But still there's fire in our souls
That glitter in your eyes
Should never fade away
No matter what your age
The youth in you should stay
Sometimes the light goes dim
And you need to make it bright
Sometimes the body gets tired
But you know you got to fight
Fight against the things
They say you can no longer do
Find a way to enjoy the child
That still lives inside of you
It's not about being silly
And jumping out of bounds
It's about understanding

How to stand firmly on the ground
Wear a smile on your face
Learn something new everyday
Cherish each moment as a blessing
Have something positive to say
Faith has helped you make this journey
Your life experience is the key
To appreciate just being here
Becomes a part of who you be
Eat the grapes from the vine
Before the fermenting starts
Take a chance and sip the wine
But always stay young at heart.

Down Time

I thrive on knowing
On having confidence
In whatever I do
Courage is my partner
We've done crazy things together
I believe in the sun
I try to shine everyday
But there are days
When rain is forecasted
And I become a dark cloud
The sun doesn't even show his face
I can't even feel him in my heart
I know he's there
Still with me
I can't see him right now
I feel cold and lonely
Detached from everything I love
Then faith smiles at me
Gives me more fuel to fight

Provides more wood for my fire
My body and soul find comfort
In the warmth of her presence
The veil of darkness is lifted
I can see clearly now
And I know this too shall past.

Anti-Superstition

I kissed a witch's tit
Turned winter into a summer's day
I took the shackles
On my wrist and ankles
And made bracelets I could sell
I took the intestines of a hog
Turned them into a delicacy
I heard the wailing screams
Made music from our pain
I took every curse
Turned it into a blessing
I turned vampire blood
Into fresh water
I took the thorn in my side
And grew a rose bush
I took a brick in my path
And built a mansion
I walked under a ladder
And found a hundred dollar bill

A black cat crossed my path
I had a lucky day
I broke a mirror
Had seven years of good fortune
I opened an umbrella inside the house
Was showered with golden nuggets
Friday the 13th
One of the luckiest days of my life
My friend and I split a pole
We're closer than we've ever been.

She dreamt of fish
And gave birth to triplets

A broom swept his feet
He spit on it
And won the lotto

If it rains on your wedding day
You'll be married forever

If you're born left handed
You're smarter than most

They crossed their fingers.

Realization

There are times
When you don't know
What you're doing
But you're doing it
You're going through the process
That you don't understand
You're committed to a project
You can't figure out
You struggle to work it out
Without knowing
It's like being in the dark
Searching for the light
Sometimes you get caught up
In the search
Until you realize
You've always had the light
It's inside of you
All you've got to do
Just turn it on.

ABIODUN OYEWOLE

Uncle Sam

They call him Uncle Sam
He dresses up in fancy clothes
Wears wigs and make up
Coats his tongue with lies
His gentlemen attitude is a disguise
For all the devilish things he does
He's portrayed as a good guy
When he's really a thug
It's a masquerade
He's playing charades
Selling hot air balloons
At the parade
Many fall for his game
See themselves as the blame
When things fall apart
Stress attacks the heart
We must uncover his plot
Find a way to stop

His demonic deeds
That make air hard to breathe
Strip him clean
Down to his soul
We'll find there's an infected hole
Spreading pain and misery
This is his legacy
Reveal his naked truth of hate
Of human kind before its too late.

Dream State

Could death be a state of dreams
Over and over again
Until your human life force is shot back
Into the universal womb of reality
We are made of body mind and soul
The body can decay like a loaf of bread
Over a period of time
The mind can lose its thought
Over a period of time
The soul lives forever
It cannot die
The soul the very essence
Of every living thing
The source of life itself
Is like the wind
It travels but never dies
When you're dreaming
Your soul is alive

With stories and events
To entertain your mind
Sometimes they seem so real
You wake up screaming
Many times I lost my car
I knew I had parked it right there
But it wasn't there
I searched all over to find it
I thought it must have been stolen
Reported it to the police
They searched too
But couldn't find it
Then I woke up
Realizing I don't even have a car
So when my body dies
And my mind becomes blank
I will dream of people places and things
I've known
Loved
And disliked in my lifetime
My dreams will go on

Like a series of movies
Until me as a sperm cell
Is shot back into orbit
To meet an egg
Another planet
So I can live this human existence
All over again.

I Seashell

I was a seashell
Lying on the beach
You found me
Picked me up
Brushed the sand off
Washed away the sand
That was inside
Put me in your bag
Took me home
I live with you now
Somewhere in the city
Far from the beach
That was my home
I feel all alone here
I'm all by myself
There are no other seashells around
Just a lot of people
Using me for an ashtray.

ABIODUN OYEWOLE

Everyday

Each day has a personality
A character of its own
A moment of reality
That I must face
Look into its eyes
And see how I can fit
How I can be
How I can live
Each morning is the same
But it is not the same
Wake up time is the same
But my feelings are not
The morning sounds
I've heard before
A police siren
A train running down the tracks
A car horn
Dogs barking
A cat in heat

The voice of my thoughts
Wondering what today might bring
So i become the audience
Of a play I am in
I have a major part
I want to be good
Giving myself a standing ovation
Everyday.

Of Worth

I feel like an ancient relic
Showered with praises
Beyond my worth
I don't feel my head
Can wear the crown
I rather have a hat
It feels good to be loved
But it scares me too
I don't think I can live
Up to all this love I've been given
But I try
I will continue to try
I don't want
To let those who love me down
I don't want to let myself down
But I am human
I make mistakes
I ask God to give me strength

I ask my ancestors
To walk by my side
God has guided me well
I have never been forsaken
I pray he will help me stand
And reflect all the good I can
Prove my worth unto myself
And always be appreciated.

An Outrage

What germ is this
That has diseased our hearts
And left our souls frozen in ice
What manner of man
Could scar the tissues of our ancestors
While they lay asleep in their graves
By abusing a child
By not holding sacred the seeds of life
What kind of being
Could kidnap a girl
And feed her to the wolves
No matter what faith
No matter what religion
No man can bless himself
While cursing the female inside of him
No matter what laws or customs
Every woman is a mother
And every mother is God

How can we damn her so
The girls were in school
Preparing to be women
Developing their minds and their bodies
Wrapped up in their innocence
They were attacked
Tide up and carted away
Like cattle on a truck
Taken to the market for slaughter
What kind of animal could do this to their own
Even the lioness will hurt the lion
Who tries to harm her young
I pray to the Gods and all of the ancestors
That lightening will strike
And thunder will roll
And a storm will come and destroy this evil
That exist in the hearts of man
So that we will once again
Praise all the forces of nature
All the trees and flowers
And let each child like a flower bloom to their fullest
Without fear of ever being uprooted or cut down

A lot of people refuse to do things because they don't want to go naked, don't want to go without guarantee. But that's what's got to happen. You go naked until you die.

~Nikki Giovanni

Of Human Interest

It seems I've become a teacher
Removed from the ashes of life
Ascended to a podium
At the head of the class
Ruled by the ruler of rules
Sometimes without reason
It seems I've become a machine
Filled with information
That I throw up
In a room full with people
Who search through this waste
Looking for food for thought
But I can still feel
I can't even help it
I have scars on my soul
From the pain that I see
And it seems that I cut myself
Just often enough
To remind me who I am

And I am only human
A tree in the forest
A bird in flight
A fish swimming in the sea of humanity
I am human
And not unlike
All of god's creations
And those I teach
Surely teach me,

Born In Water

We were born in water
Yet many don't know how to swim
Some are afraid of the water
The very source of our being
Is a major fear in our lives
Water is the passion of the gods
Without all that heat
Water can put a fire out
It can make the sky weep
Water is the purification
Of our minds bodies and souls
The value of water
Out weighs the value of gold
We sweat when we work hard
We spit when we've had enough
Although water is soft
Water is also tough
We are baptized in water
So our spirits will be reborn

Water is the holy ointment from god
That washes our sins away
Water is the transport of our energy
And the wellness of our being.

Cyn Control Your Nigger

The nigger was a character
Created for those they had enslaved
Just like a mule was a hybrid
This is how a nigger was made
Take a black man out of Africa
Forbid him to speak his language too
Treat him like he was an animal
And have him do what you want him to do
For over four hundred years
Kidnapped blacks have been called niggers
Part of a plan for blacks to hate themselves
Over the years the nigger has gotten bigger
And many blacks are living in hell
English was the language given
That blacks in America were forced to speak
We had to change our way of living

But never were we weak
We took the language and gave it meanings
You couldn't find in a dictionary
Like the sun our creativity is beaming
Saying that we're extraordinary
Bad was no longer negative
To us it meant very, very good
And nigger is what we called each
Other in the neighborhood
It was really how you said it
More than a word it was the tone
So many folks don't really get it
You see we've made this English our own
Now if you're acting out of order
A nigger might be what you're called
To help you get it together
Before you take a fall
The nigger is a character
That we have all come to know
He doesn't work well with others
He won't help flowers grow
But the nigger can be a weapon

You may have to use from time to time
You must control your nigger
Or else he'll make you lose your mind
Control requires discipline
In what we say and do
We can not live as wild as the wind
If we want our dreams to come true
Your day to day activities
Should make it clear that you're black
You only use your nigger when your black is under attack
This poem is for all of those
Who understand the nigger roar
Inside each of us lives a nigger
That we must control for sure.

She Didn't Know

She was a natural beauty
But she didn't know that
Smooth satin black skin
That glistened in the sunlight
The trees would smile
When she walked by
She didn't know that
The birds would sing
Songs for her
Flowers would blossom
In her presence
She didn't know that
So she bleached her skin
Wore false eyelashes
Died her hair blonde
Idolized white girls
When white girls
Wished they looked
Like her
But she didn't know that.

ABIODUN OYEWOLE

Guilty

I too am guilty
I have lied
To myself and others
I have stretched the truth
Beyond boundaries of its existence
And yet my truth has more value
The lies are cheats and cheap
It seems make believe
Is more accepted
Truth is always
More exciting than fiction
Still I've lied
To impress
To glorify the unholy
To stake claim
To something I could never possess
And like all who are guilty
I too must pay
I too must suffer the consequences

Eat this bitter fruit
Lay on this bed of nails
Wash my face in mud
I am not a saint
Just a human
With weak links in my chain

ABIODUN OYEWOLE

God Call

The older I get
The more I call on god
He's always been here
In my youth
I took him for granted
Time has made me see
Midnight will come
Dawn will be a memory
So I call on god
To help me make it through
To give me joy
In these last years
To offer peace to my soul
To provide love for my heart
Each breath is more precious now
Every action is more conscious
My heart beat is like a drum
Beating louder every step I take
The older I get

My inner vision is more clear
I see yesterday in tomorrow
And hold sacred the present
Love becomes a prayer that I worship
Gratitude becomes the mission of my life.

My Desire

To see your face
And hold you in my arms
To press your lips against mine
And feel your tongue
Touching and flirting
With my tongue
To feel warm all over
As I stand erect
Wanting you
Caressing you
Tasting you
Sucking your nipples
While my hand explores
The valley of your soul
Where worlds are created
That sacred place
I resided for nine months
To feel your softness

And stretch in the soil of your earth
To look into your eyes
And know that we are flying
Above the clouds
That try to consume us
This is my desire
This is my dream.

At This Moment

It is moments like these
That I wish you were here
Where I could touch you
And feel your lips
Pressed against mine
Look into your eyes and know
That we are here
In the same place
At the same time together
Even beyond the distance
There is a spirit
That lovers share
Like a soft breeze
Blowing through the limbs
Of a naked tree
There are feelings
That can't be denied
Like a fire burning

Deep in your soul

Enough passion to melt an iceberg

I feel the heat

I embrace the heat

And comfort my soul

With the light of your love.

ABIODUN OYEWOLE

Out of Sorts

Sometimes things are just out of sync
It's difficult to go to sleep at night
And day light doesn't make things easier to see
You feel like you're in a fog
And you can't see in front of you
You review your past
Trying to recapture a moment
That put you back on solid ground
But it's like the wind that goes by
Never to return the same way
You try hard to remember
What you did to make you proud
What you did to make you happy
But all you see are clouds and rain
All you hear are babies crying
In the back of your mind
Why do I feel like this
What have I done

To make me visit the basement of my life
And drape my being in sadness
Thinking about all the good things I've lost
All the good people I've known
Even the music in my soul brings me down
Happiness seems so far away
And loneliness is my closet companion
I must find a way out
I must summon all my strength
And find the sun that's hiding
Somewhere inside of me
I must make him shine
So I will know
All is not lost
And what is lost can be found
I must keep the faith in my heart
For that is all that I have left.

I've Been Down

I've been down before
I know what it looks like
In the cellar of my soul
I have felt the chill of neglect
And the fear of wondering
If I'll be here tomorrow
Depression has tried to embrace me
And confine me to a dark corner
And we have battled
I always win
But not without doubt
Not without scars
From a fight for my life
I have had days
When I thought I'd never smile again
I've been down before
But I know how to get up
I know when it's time to end

My poor pity party
My feelings are real and deep as any well
But I try to remember
The well leads to a stream
And there I'll find my dreams
To keep me up
And not be down too long.

I Am Water

I am the rain
That falls from the sky
I am the tears
From a baby's eyes
I am the streams
Running over the rocks
I am the waterfalls
Cascading from mountain tops
I am the rivers
Where fresh water is found
I am the ocean
Leaving salt on the ground
I am seventy five percent
Of what lives inside man
I am three quarters
Of this earth our land
I am the blood
Of mother earth

Making everything flow
I am liquid sun
Helping everything grow
Come tell me your story
See yourself in me
I am the reflection
Of life
I was born to be free.

ABIODUN OYEWOLE

It's Not Easy

Sometimes I've got to swim
Against the current
Go against the grain
Lift myself up
From the bottom of my feet
And try not to go insane
No it's not easy
But somehow I do it
Somehow I find a way to cruise
Across the sea
When it should be a struggle
Somehow I rearrange the grain
And find a way to carve my name
And then spread my arms
Toward the sky
And command my feet and mind to fly
But the gods know
It's not easy.

Contemplation

I often sit and stare at the sky
And the buildings beneath it
It is the sky that makes me wonder
That triggers my imagination
The vastness of that sky
Sometimes blue
Sometimes gray
But it covers everything
Its presence can't be denied
And somehow it houses
All our dreams and wishes
All of our secrets and plans
The sky knows them
And provides shelter for a lonely soul
Lifts us up off the ground of our feelings
And gives us faith that we too can fly.

The Formula

Before you can tell someone
To put their house in order
You've got to put your house in order
You can't chastise
Until you recognize
You have to look at yourself
Before you criticize someone else
Sometimes it's an excuse
That we point fingers at the abuse
Without looking inside
At what we've tried to hide
It all starts with you
Unto yourself you must be true
You can't play the blame game
And wear the clothes of shame
What part did you play
That led you astray
Were you blind deaf and dumb

And had no clue of where it was coming from
We must first go inside ourselves and see
Who we are
And who we want to be
We must take control of our lives
So our dreams can be realized
It's our responsibility
To safe guard ourselves from misery
To protect the sacredness of our being
And question everything we're seeing
Beware of the poison
That looks and taste like candy
Beware of the gifts
That could be a trap
Stand firm in your beliefs
Stay on your path
Take no shortcuts
Only then will you know success
Only then will you be at your best.

A Somber Day

It's a somber day
Gray skies no sun
Not even a bird flying by
The trees have lost their clothes
Standing there naked
In my sight
Like skeletons in a science class
No skin to cover their bones
And I poet see them
From my window
And I wonder
Could they be me
When I'm not so sure
Of who or what I am
Am I looking in the mirror
Exposing myself
Of who I thought I was
Not beating my drum
To announce my presence

On this planet
So I wrap myself in memories
Of those I've loved
And those who loved me
And I wait for the rain to fall
Or the sun to shine.

For Our Lives

We have years behind us
But we still look ahead
Age has become the seasoning
For our lives
Life taste even better now
The body doesn't do
All the things it used to do
So we make sure our steps
Safeguard our movements
And we live on
Our minds have taken us places
Our bodies could never go
Our spirit is the very air we breathe
Life is more precious now
Relationships are more sacred
We are that fine wine
More potent with time
There are good things

That come with age
There are revelations
That make us see more clearly
We've become familiar
With the cycle
We recognize each round a little better
The youth in us has not died
It's that ray of light on an overcast day.

"Naked poetry, always mine, / that I
have loved my whole life!"

~Juan Ramón Jiménez

We Be Naked

We come to this world
Naked
Our bare body
Baring our bare souls and minds
Stripped of all earthly things
A being unto ourselves
With not even words
To use as a cover
As time moves on
We are dressed
With fabrics and tags
And opinions of who
And why we are
We are neither pink nor blue
We just are
We are given garments
To define us
We are given names
To claim us

We are given thoughts
To think for us
I want to return to naked
Allow my spirit to be the only thing I wear.

The Meaning

What does it mean
The signs are there
I can't read them
I know they speak to me
I can't understand
What they're saying
It seems my soul is deft
I only hear music
The drums are loud
The silence is louder
What does it mean
How can I cope
What hope do I have
Of being alright
Of reaching my goals
I need love by my side
She comes in a dream
I wake up sweating alone

My brain is on fire
I might explode
At any moment
I remember when I was a child
I felt the same way
What does it mean
Am I traveling backwards
Trying to look ahead
To a future
That's already happened.

A Small Act

What does it cost
To be kind to someone
An act of kindness
Can go a long way
To hold the door
For someone who is coming
To say good morning
And have a nice day
To smile when someone smiles at you
To excuse me please and thank you
Carries a lot of weight
In a world of tight lips and cold stares
To apologize when you've done something wrong
To call a friend
Let them know you were thinking about them
To offer a seat to an elder
Or a woman with a baby
How much does that cost
Kindness has no price

To look in someone's eyes
And tell them you care
To give flowers to your mother
To share good news
To give good advice when asked
Just a small act of kindness
Something we should never forget
It makes the sun shine bright
Even on a cloudy day.

It's Me

For much too long
I've looked outside myself
Trying to find answers
Trying to connect the dots
Just to find the treasure
That was hidden in me
All along
But now I know
I am the wealth of my life
The deliverer of my gift
No one has the responsibility
For my success or failures
But me
No one can determine
How far I'll go
But me
No one can give me peace of mind
But me

And yet I still stand in line
Waiting for my time
To serve or be served
Waiting for my number to pop up
For my name to be called
When I hold the keys
To the locked doors around me
All I've got to do
Use my mind and my will
To unlock the doors
To get out of the box
And fly
I guess I'm afraid of heights.

A Tear for an Artist

I wish I could creep inside of you
Turn the lights on
It seems so dark in there
Maybe I would find a way
Open up the curtains
Raise the shades
So the sun could shine through
You guru woman
With a paint brush
Bringing light to others
You've come to adjust your eyes
To the dimness
The clouds seem to consume you
But there's no rain in sight
You're a blues song
In the middle of a celebration
Where everyone is dancing
You're dragging your soul across the floor
I pray for your return to the light

I pray for day
When you will smile again
And shine like the star
You were meant to be.

ABIODUN OYEWOLE

Love is Ageless

Love is ageless
It's forever reborn
In the hearts and souls of lovers
It is the spark
That lights the flame
To give passion a tongue
Lips and hands to feel
Love is the music
That makes you dance
The song you want to sing
The joy that lifts your spirit
That uncut diamond
Created by years of pressure
Love will always endure
A thousand years may go by
Love remains the same
Like a child that never grows old
But embraces the wisdom of age

Like the sun that always shines
Even through a dark and dreary storm
Love is there
Love is the presence of god
Living inside of us
That we can see
In the eyes of each other.

Affirmation

You are beautiful
It's not how you look
It's how you feel
You are intelligent
It's not how you think
It's what you do
When you use control
Of your mind
Nothing and no one
Can break you down
You are stronger
Than your enemies
Your roots are deeper
Your ancestors are always with you
You will never be defeated
You will learn when you lose
You will gain more
Because you know

Even on a cloudy day
You bring out the sun
Even when it rains
Each raindrop is filled with nutrients
To make you stronger
You are the antidote
To the pain they try to give you
You are powerful
The god in you is almighty
You carry pyramids
In your pockets
Diamonds in your mind
And gold in your soul
This makes you richer than most
You are beautiful.

I Am Not Afraid

I'm walking through the wilderness
With wild animals all around
I step over bodies
That have been mauled
I see body parts
Lying in my path
I hear screams
Watch tears fall
From the leaves of trees
But I am not afraid
Sometimes I have to walk
Around puddles of blood
Hold my nose
From the smell of human guts
Hanging from tree limbs
But I am not afraid
I smell the human bodies
Burning in the fire
I taste the foul air

The victims of wildebeests
I hear the beasts growling
Feel their footsteps getting closer
But I am not afraid
Sometimes I stop walking
Find a smooth rock to sit on
And wait for the beasts
To come my way
They come i see them
They see me
They walk on by
I sit there looking at them
Wondering where did they go wrong
I am very calm
I have no fear of being harmed
Because I am not afraid.

Moment of Prayer

This is a moment of prayer
For all of those who struggle
For all of those who wonder
How they make it from day to day
This is a moment of prayer
To pay respect
To bear witness
To the task that lies ahead
This task is called life
Life here borders on death
Smiles don't come easily
Joy is not in the air we breathe
Happiness seems so far away
Still we struggle
Trying to make this life liveable
Trying to hurdle all the obstacles
Gracefully
Telling ourselves

It's gonna be alright
We want to believe
This is a moment of prayer
To give strength to our faith
Wisdom to our courage
We are gods children
All prayers will be answered.

Feeling Lonely

There are times
When you feel alone
Almost abandoned
Like an orphan child
Sitting on a park bench
With only the trees
And the birds chirping
For company
Or maybe you're on a crowded train
With hundreds of strangers
And no one to talk to
No one to laugh with
In this sea of humanity
You feel all alone
No one to ask you
How you feel
And no one to listen
To what you have to say

You can even hear the music
But no one to dance with
There are times
In our loneliness
We daydream
About the fun days
And all the friends we had
Like the leaves of a tree
That have fallen
And like the tree
We are left naked
To the eyes of the world
And you think about your friends
And you wonder if they are lonely too
Do they miss you
Like you miss them
But it's not your time to go
You have more to do
You'll get over this moment
And continue your search to be happy.

Fear

It's about fear
It's about your heart beating out of rhythm
And your nerves on fire
It's about hiding in the corner of your mind
Fighting back thoughts
That try to invade the calm
And fear is laughing
Is rearing his head back and laughing
While you turn yourself inside out
Looking for a safe place to disappear
But fear got you
He put his hand on your shoulder
For one moment
Your breathing stopped
And with your eyes wide open
In broad daylight
You visit all of your nightmares
Watch your dreams turn to ashes

And your heart put on ice
Fear becomes a virus
Infecting your soul
Causing you to forget your history
And how you always made it through
Fear didn't reside on your block then
Nobody even knew who he was
But the devil needed toys
And fear was his playmate
And everyone was invited
To his circus
To ride on his scary-go-round
But when the roller coaster crashed
And the haunted house caught on fire
And the children drowned in the pool
And the cotton candy was laced with cyanide
Fear stepped in
And snatched the hearts out of chests
Of those who thought that life always had a happy ending
But one day we'll wake up and realize
Fear ain't nothing but a bad dream.

Homeless

New York City
The showcase city of America
Where people from around the world
Come to be dazzled
By the sights and sounds of the city
The plays the concert halls
The stores the theaters the clubs
The restaurants
And the crowds
The city that never sleeps
Becomes a challenge
For residents and visitors
But the city is not paved in gold
Homeless people decorate the streets
Sit on sidewalks on corners
Like a lampost that has no light bulb
Asking for spare change
Holding cardboard signs

That say "I'm hungry"
Here in this city
With too much of everything
How can people starve
There is an eatery on every block
How could people be homeless
There are new skyscrapers
That will never be completely occupied
Being erected every day
How can any human being
Watch another human being suffer
To see someone else lose touch
With the humanity of themselves
And be reduced
To the level of a stray dog
Looking through garbage for food
This is an open sore that needs healing
There is a shatter dream
That needs mending
Somehow the god in each of us
Must find a way to deliver.

Father Time

Of all the fathers we know
There's only one who will always show
He'll never leave you behind
And he's known as father time
He stays with you from birth
While you're on this planet earth
For better or for worse
He can be a blessing or a curse
Father time is always moving
He only stops at his own choosing
He's much bigger than any clock
He can give or take away everything you got
He may let your star shine today
And allow the world to see your light
He can make it fade away
And turn all your days into nights
Father time brings changes
To your body mind and soul
If you try and disrespect him

He'll let you rot and turn to mold
So you must recognize his presence
He won't be cheated and you can't lie
He'll help you make your dreams come true
Or make a way for you to die.

ABIODUN OYEWOLE

Death & Funerals

He has a fiendish grin
And always dresses in black
His teeth are rotten
His voice is raspy
Some call him the grim reaper
Doesn't like sunlight
Dark clouds are his sky
His friends are sickness and depression
War and misery
Hates music
Loves pain
He has bad breath
His favorite toys are guns and bombs
Poison , lies and hate
His body gives off a stench
You can smell a mile away
He is persuasive and very greedy
And doesn't have any manners
His parties are called funerals

Where he loves to play the organ
And watch people drown their face in tears
Some have become intimate with him
And wear him like jewels around their neck
Grief and mourning are his cousins
They provide entertainment
At his funerals
None of us come here to die
We grow to live and love more everyday
Even when he takes us by the hand
And brings us to the party
We come to celebrate life
We come to witness his cocoon
Turn into a colorful butterfly
We dance and sing to praise the person
Riding on the winds of change
And with love we send their spirits
To another form of creation
Life is an eternal passion
That death could never replace
But momentarily interferes with our day.

ABIODUN OYEWOLE

Hey Fly

(poem inspired by my friend Fikisha)

Hey fly
It's just you and I
Only you can get away
But I have to stay
You see I'm locked up
And I can't get the key
But you on the other hand
Are always free
You know you get on my nerves
Flying around in my face
I take swipes at you
Messing with my space
You're tiny
And you land
Where ever you like
I guess I look like a giant
In your sight
They say you have a short life

But you've been around forever
Do you come back the same
Are you affected by the weather
Do you fly south in the winter
And come back in the spring
Are you a short distance sprinter
And what message do you bring
Yes fly I would like to know
Do you represent
The high and the low.

Be Still

Can we be still for a moment
Can we turn off the volume
In our minds
Embrace our solitude
There is a volcano
Erupting in the world
Can we chill and not panic
Hot lava is everywhere
Can we learn
How to walk in space
We've heard the screams
We've seen the bodies
We want to live
We want to love
We must be still
Allow our hearts
To provide the music
Allow our imagination
To provide the show

Only when we are still
Quiet within ourselves
Will we hear mother nature
And the message
That she brings
Her message is in her song
Her song is in the wind
The wind is the breath
We breathe
We are forever.

Alone

I am here all alone
Even with a crowd around me
I am in solitude with myself
My body feels their presence
My soul and mind are on an island
I spend my time talking to trees
Singing to flowers
Praying to rocks and the sky
And sometimes I just talk to myself
I am here alone and lonely
Splashing in puddles on planet Neptune
Counting the ripples in the water
Feeling the breeze brush against my soul
I want to connect with other living things
I am a child of nature
A leaf on a tree that out lasted all the others
I am caught up in my aloneness
Solitaire is the only game I play.

Naked Poetry . . . that is, poetry without any dress, without any ornament, the very essence or body of poetry unveiled by artifice of any kind.

~Lafcadio Hearn

My Pain Is My Glory

I've been beaten down
To the ground
Bruises on my body and face
Blood dripping from my lip
Even my tooth was knocked out of place

But I got up and fought back
It's part of my legacy
Because I'm black

I've had bombs dropped on me
And I was shot
While I laid asleep in my bed
Now I'm a panther set free
Because of the people
I'll never be dead

I got up and fought back
It's part of my legacy
Because I'm black

I've been locked up in jail
And hung from a tree
I used the time to not fail
And that tree has become me
I've been castrated, miseducated
And segregated too
But I'm educated and celebrated
For all the wonderful things I do
You see I don't like pain
But it makes me strong
It seems rather insane
That I could make right from wrong

I got up and fought back
It's part of my legacy
Because I'm black.

Each Day

We arise each morning
With the sun
Give thanks to our creator
That this day has come
We pray and sit in meditation
To make good decisions
To fulfill our dedication
Each day presents a challenge
That we try to accept
There are deeds and promises
We know must be kept
Sometimes it's a struggle
Sometimes it is not
What we need to succeed
We've already got
There are many distractions
That can throw us off course
When we clear the air
We realize we have the force

The power of god resides in our souls
As long as we believe
We can't lose control
So we set our sites
And start on our mission
At the end of the day we make clear our vision.

Hush

I talk too much
I'm tired of hearing
The sound of my voice
I want to be quiet
Inside and out
I want to be in a space
And make no sound
Just listen to my thoughts
Sometimes my thoughts are so loud
They dwarf the sound of my voice
I don't even want to hear me singing
I love to sing
I just want to hear the music
In my soul
Let it play for my mind and body
To be inspired
To do something wonderful
Something that will last longer
Then a sound bite

Something that will make people see
And take notice
Without letting words
Get in the way.

Empty

I am empty right now
All of who I thought I was
Has been poured out
Leaving me vacant
Even the walls
Of my soul are bare
I am just space
With nothing to define me
I thought I had so much
I thought I was full
With promise and love
With talents and gifts
But there's nothing now
I am just a hole
In the middle of a donut
I can't even collect the air
I have nothing to hold it
The wind has more body than me

I don't exist
I have ceased to be
My hopes and dreams and wishes
Have evaporated
I am left without
All I thought I knew.

Body Clock

There are some things
I'd like to do
But I can't do them
Any more
I've run out of time
My body doesn't perform
Like it used to
Age has become
My arresting officer
He has confined
My movements
He has restricted
My activity
I am left
With only dreams
And memories
The physical energy
Is not the same

Climbing stairs
Has become a chore
I take a break
When I'm walking
It's hard to believe
My body has betrayed me
Breathing
Has become an effort
I am not waiting to die
There is more life in me
There are
Creative juices
Flowing
Through my veins
I must respond
So I ask the gods
And my ancestors
To make me stronger
And give me more time.

Fulfillment

I try to be strong
And carry this weight
The weight of life
Of living a life
That I have created for myself
I have chosen my path
Or maybe this path has chosen me
I want to succeed
Feasting off the fruit of my labor
Some might say
I am a success
I've withstood the fire
Used the flames for light
To see how far I can go
To discover how much I can do
But sometimes I feel weak
Afraid of the shadows
That follow me

Even when the sun is shinning
I know so much
I know so little
There is so much more to learn
Let the lessons continue
I remain a student
In the class of mother nature
She'll tell me in the wind
She'll show me in the sky
She'll touch me in the rain
I will keep growing
Until I return
Back to the beginning.

Evil

Evil is here

Evil never died

He took a short nap

And woke up with a vengeance

Everything good did

He wants to destroy

He's called out all his friends

They are ready to battle

They got the guns

The twisted look on their faces

Cursing god with all the symbols of hate

Marching down the street

They are looking for a fight

With clubs and shields and flags

Proclaiming their right to be sick

And the people protest

To ears that can't hear

And eyes that can't see

To the powers that be
Evil has allies in government
They eat raw flesh
And drink blood together
They relish in the suffering of others
Evil wants to rule the world
Wants to see people starving
Homeless and crazy
Evil is entertained
By the pain and madness they bring
They are thrilled to see death
To smell flesh burning
And see bloodshed
Evil can't be killed
He can't die
But he can be recognized
He can be left to drown and suffocate
In his own feces and piss.

Soul Dive

Sometimes I dive into
The depths of my soul
To discover the task
The gods have in store for me
I hold my breath
Close my eyes
Dive head first into
The well of my soul
Allow my spirit to breathe for me
Hold on to faith
That I will safely return
I am not afraid
I am willing to let go
Knowing the truth will be my guide
I am strong enough
But I am weak at the same time
Strong enough to face the truth
Weak enough to submit

I know I have been blessed
My blessings are deeds
I must work to fulfill
This is my road
No one travels this way but me
I travel alone
Sometimes meeting up with a friend
Sometimes meeting up with a foe
I must recognize the difference
And move on down the road
Make progress in spite of
The road blocks in my path
The anointment of my soul
Will help me along the way
My soul is the essence of God
Living inside of me
Clearly telling me
What I should do
I am learning how to listen
To take heed
And always walk toward the light.

In a Bubble

Sometimes I'm in a bubble
Just floating above the ground
Not connected to anyone or anything
Caught up in myself
My thoughts
My feelings
My world
I sometimes wonder
Why I feel this way
If I were not in this body
In this space and time
Would I still think like this
Would I still feel like this
And yet I seek the love of another
The desire to be wanted
But still I'm alone
In the middle of a crowd
I don't feel connected

Like a strange bush in the forest
Surrounded by tall trees
And other plants and flowers
I stand out
I stand alone
No one thinks like me
No one feels like me
And yet I must find a way
To be in concert
To be connected
Or float away in my bubble
Where not even I can find me.

Slavery

How did this come to be
A life of slavery
Africans were captured chained and whipped
Then forced to get on those slave ships
Stripped of their names
Culture and identity
Reduced to nothing
Not even a memory
Slept naked with chains in bowels and piss
No human being had ever been through this
Sharks followed the boats
They knew they'd get a meal
Of those who were sick
And those who wouldn't yield
The middle passage crossed the Atlantic
The beginning of a saga painfully tragic
Africans kidnapped
Brought to the new world

Precious cargo
Worth more than diamonds and pearls
Given new names
Had nothing to claim
Treated like animals
Driven insane
For four hundred years
Africans tried to survive
Through abuse and torture
Many lost their lives
When the chains were broken
And Africans were set free
They had to create a new life
Just so they could be
They tried to show pride
And shine like a star
But the slavery experience
Left everlasting scars
It caused many to hate
The color of their skin
And make many think
We were never born to win

The effort to heal
Continues today
To shed all the shackles
And be the prayers that we pray.

Loud Silence

The quiet is so loud
The noise of my thoughts
Is killing me
The silence is an echo of death
I am becoming deaf
With the sound of my heart
Beating louder
Than thirty drummers
Beating on pots and pans
I need to hear her voice
I need to know
I am not alone
It's like I've been locked up
In solitary confinement
In a world with nine million people
Around me.

Blood Rite

The Nile flows through me
It's the blood of my ancestors
It's the stream of life's beginnings
Is the passageway to freedom
Is the juice of all living things
My soul swims in the currents
Of my legacy
And I am old
But young enough to grow
They have tried to pollute me
Stunt my growth
Drown me in the sea of myself
But I swim on
Just like the Nile upstream
Going against all odds
Doing what some say is impossible
It was my blood that made the water salty
It was the milk from my mother's breast

That nurtured the world
I was born to be here
And live my life in paradise
It's my blood rite

Audacity

Yes it's true
I do what I do
I was born to be free
I came to earth to be me
I can't be stopped
And I'm ready to rock
This world with my pen
I'm a blessing not a sin
I know how to win
From the beginning to the end
I tell the story right
I know how to fight
With all the weapons I got
My voice is like a gunshot
You see my tongue is the trigger
To lash out at a nigger
I got an arsenal of words
I make revolution an action verb

To set fire to your ass
I can be crude or use class
This ain't no joke
I've always been dope
When I was a kid
The things I said and did
Seem to cause waves
I've always been brave
Serious about change
Driving my enemies insane
Making them all realize
My people are the prize
No one has our swag nor our love
It comes naturally
It's nothing you have to think of
They build walls to contain
Try to make me feel ashame
I turn the wall into art
What they think is the end
Is just the start
Of a world revolution
I am the solution

I'm strapped and packed
And undoubtedly black
I know the truths I got the facts
And know how to act
I know how to shine
I'm one of a kind
You see I have the capacity
To accommodate my audacity.

Just a Kiss

It was just a kiss
The feel of her lips
Pressed against mine
The taste of her breath
Music for our tongues to dance
It was just a kiss
That made me feel warm inside
Made me believe
True love never dies
Made me think
How deserted my mouth would be
Without her kiss
Painting lavender in my soul
Letting me know
No matter what
God will always be with us
Even if it's for just a kiss

Forgiveness

How do we forgive those
Who abuse and use us
Who have a thrill to kill us
Who take and rape us
Time and time again
Are we more Christian than Christ
To watch our sons and daughters
Being slaughtered
And we embrace this pain
That drives us insane
It seems we blame ourselves
For living in hell
With some strange desire
To be consumed by fire
While the devil smiles
Eating a happy meal
Caring not how we feel at all
We take the fall

Then make the call to god
We spare the rod
What happened to an eye for an eye
A tooth for a tooth
Could it be the truth
Is too much to bare
So we settle for a prayer.

My Prayer

I want to reach down into my soul
And find the feeling
That I can express
In a poem
In a song
In a conversation
I want to dive deep
Into the well of my blackness
And find the right words
The right sound
To uplift those around me
Those who hear me
And be a reflection of a blessing
That only prayers and meditation can bring
I want mother nature
To take me by the hand
And walk with me
Through her garden
Bathe in the sun showers

And watch the buds blossom
Into leaves and flowers
Let the spring breeze tell me secrets
Of ways I can use my magic
I want to age like good wine
And be more potent as I get older.

A Reminder

Curiosity is the seed of intelligence
Knowledge is his only companion
When the children want to know
Asking questions help them grow
To understand something new
Is what adults are suppose to do
Take time to explain
And show them how to use their brain
Make thinking the only game
They can play
Like sponges they absorb
What we do and say
Each child may have a different interest
Each child may have a different taste
We must help them make the connections
To everything that they will face
Some may move in circles
Others may move in a square
Some are swift

Some move like turtles
They both will make it
If we show we really care

Salvation

We must save ourselves
Or live and die in hell
Stop the fires from raging
Be more engaging
Let love be our light
To make everything right
Hate is so strong
It celebrates what's wrong
We can put this fire out
We don't have to shout
Allow the god inside of you
To help you do what you need to do
Where each breath
Is no longer a sacrifice
We're on a mission to create a paradise
Build a bond between each other
Share and care for one another
Throw away the lies
Live in the truth

Wear no disguise
Let your light be the proof
We were born to shine
And save each other from harm
Humanity is in trouble
Let's sound the alarm.

A Year Without You

It's been a year since you've been gone
And it's still hard to believe you're gone
You meant so much to me
And you still do
I lived to love you
To be with you
To share a poem with you
Or a new song
To get advice from you
To help me see my way
Through this maze of life
That we all seem to be caught up in
You were my time out
My refuge
My comfort
My sanctuary
From the conflicts shortcomings and disappointments
I sometimes had to face

You were my air filter
To give me fresh air to breathe
I miss sharing a meal with you
And the way you could mix a drink
And your smile
And words of encouragement
Were the gifts you shared
That made me feel secure
And create something new
To be happy here on earth
No matter how bad or sad
Things seem to be.

All Dressed Up

I watched the trees
Get dressed today
They wore a light green garment
Giving flavor to the park
Under the background
Of a baby blue sky
I listened to the sounds
Of children playing
In the trees living room
Everyone seemed happy
Now that the trees
Were no longer naked
Exposing their skin and bones
They were putting on clothes
Getting ready for the summer festivities
I could even smell the barbecue
Cooking on the grill
I could hear the music

From a boom box
The flowers were dancing
And the birds were singing
Letting us know
Spring hand finally sprung.

We Are Survivors

The legacy of my people
Has no equal
We've always been divine
And a gift to mankind
Snatched from our native land
Put on slave ships
Treated like animals
Beaten with a bullwhip
Naked and chained together
Across the Atlantic we came
To live and die a slave
Many were scarred and maimed
Some of us died
And took our own lives
But through it all
Most of us survived
Being chained on a ship
Sitting in our own bowels and piss
How strong we had to be

To survive all of this
Then to be auctioned and sold
Like a piece of furniture
Our spirits remained unbroken
They had no clue who we were
So we picked cotton and cut cane
And lived in a shack
Ate the scraps from a pig
But no disease did we attract
Thousands of natives were killed
By the disease called small pox
Somehow blacks survived
We were the one s god had not forgot
After six hundred years of being here
We've seen diseases come and go
Some of us have died
Most of us found ways to grow
After slavery they tried to kill us
Anyway they could
So they became a human disease
Covered in sheets wearing a hood

Many of us were hung shot
Or beat to death
But our lives are like the wind
We are the best of god's breath
It seems the slave merchants
Didn't know
Just how precious their cargo was
Despite everything they did to kill us
We still showered the world
With love
It seems every generation
Has to deal with a new disease
Instead of us dying
We're multiplying
And enjoying the growth
Of our seeds
We work with mother nature
And our ancestors protect us to
We're here on earth
To make a difference
In the things we say and do

The legacy of my people
Has no equal
We've always been divine
And a gift to all mankind.

Life

That which is most precious
More sacred than anything
We call it life
To hear a baby cry
To feel a soft summer breeze
Brush against your face
To watch the sunrise and set
To taste the sweetness of a grape
To hear the chirping of birds
Watch the trees grow leaves
To feel the cool waters of a stream
Rush across your naked feet
To listen to music you desire
To kiss the lips of your lover
To feel the passion
A warm sensation all through your body
To embrace each other
Close to your heart
Feel the pulse of their soul

Even when they're not there
To appreciate all the flowers
The variety of color
The reds the yellows pinks purples oranges greens
Blues and whites
To decorate your space
With their presence
To hear the sound of a voice
That soothes your mind
A song that makes you smile
To hear laughter
That comes from the heart
To watch the clouds
Move across the sky
To reveal the baby blue of the day
To see the face of the one you love
To know that they love you too
This is life
And the joy of living.

I place my fingers upon these keys
typing 2,000 dreams per minute
and naked of spirit dance forth my
cosmic vortex upon this crucifix called
language.

~Aberjhani

NAKED QUOTES

HERE ARE BRIEF biographies of the individuals quoted throughout NAKED:

> *Nakedness has no color: this can come as news only to those who have never covered, or been covered by, another naked human being.*
> *~James Baldwin*

JAMES BALDWIN (1924-1987) was an African American novelist, playwright, essayist, poet, and activist. Baldwin's essays, novels, short stories, and plays fictionalize fundamental personal questions and dilemmas amid complex social and psychological pressures. One of the twentieth century's greatest writers, Baldwin broke literary ground with the exploration of racial and social issues in his many works.

> *Facts which at first seem improbable will, even on scant explanation, drop the cloak which has hidden them and stand forth in naked and simple beauty. ~Galileo Galilei*

GALILEO GALILEI (1564-1642) was an Italian astronomer, mathematician, physicist, philosopher and professor who made pioneering observations of nature with long-lasting implications for the study of physics. His inventions included the telescope, and his discoveries laid the foundation for modern physics and astronomy. Galileo was accused twice of heresy by the church for his beliefs, and wrote a number of books on his ideas. (p. 7)

> *A lot of people refuse to do things because they don't want to go naked, don't want to go without guarantee. But that's what's got to happen. You go naked until you die.* ~Nikki Giovanni

NIKKI GIOVANNI (1943) is an African American poet, writer, commentator, activist, and educator who gained initial fame in the late 1960s as one of the foremost poets of the Black Arts Movement. Her poetry anthologies, poetry recordings, and nonfiction essays, covers topics ranging from race and social issues to children's literature. She has won numerous awards, including the Langston Hughes Medal and the NAACP Image Award, and has been named as one of Oprah Winfrey's 25 "Living Legends." (p. 37)

> *"Naked poetry, always mine, / that I have loved my whole life!"* ~Juan Ramón Jiménez

JUAN RAMÓN JIMÉNEZ (1881-1958) was a Spanish poet and prolific writer. He belonged to a group of writers who, calling themselves *modernistas,* and staged a literary revival in the wake of Spain's loss of her colonies to the United States (1898). By the 1920s, Ramón Jiménez became the acknowledged master of the new generation of poets whose poetic output during his life was immense. He received the Nobel Prize in Literature in 1956 for his lyrical poetry, which in the Spanish language constitutes an example of high spirit and artistical purity. (p. 71)

> *Naked Poetry . . . that is, poetry without any dress, without any ornament, the very essence or body of poetry unveiled by artifice of any kind.* ~Lafcadio Hearn

LAFCADIO HEARN (1850-1904) was a Greek-born writer, translator, poet and teacher. He also published under the Japanese name Koizumi Yakumo, and introduced the culture and literature of Japan to the West. Hearn grew up in Dublin, studied in England and France, immigrated to the United States at age nineteen and became a newspaper reporter. He worked as a correspondent in the French West Indies, and eventually went to Japan where he would remain for the rest of his life. His articles and essays covered a wide range of topics, including politics and race relations. He published novels, and is best known for informative short stories, haiku and specifically, ghost stories about the customs, religion, and literature of Japan. (p. 107)

> *I place my fingers upon these keys typing 2,000 dreams per minute and naked of spirit dance forth my cosmic vortex upon this crucifix called language.* ~Aberjhani

ABERJHANI (1957) is an African American historian, columnist, novelist, poet, artist, and editor. Although well known for his blog articles on literature and politics, he is perhaps best known as co-author of *Encyclopedia of the Harlem Renaissance* and author of *The River of Winged Dreams.* The encyclopedia won a Choice Academic Title Award in 2004. Aberjhani served as coeditor of the *Savannah Literary Journal,* literary reviewer for the Georgia Council for the Arts and held various positions with the Poetry Society of Georgia, the oldest literary organization in the state. He has become well known as both a spoken word poet and published author. (p, 157)◙

ABOUT THE POET

PHOTO: © Chester Higgins Archives

ABIODUN OYEWOLE is a poet, teacher, and founding member of the American music and spoken-word group, The Last Poets (established in 1968), which laid the groundwork for the emergence of hip hop. He performed on The Last Poets' albums, *The Last Poets* (1970), *Holy Terror* (1993), and *The Time Has Come* (1997). Oyewole rejoined The Last Poets during its 1990s resurgence, and co-authored with Umar Bin Hassan, *On A Mission: Selected Poems and a History of The Last Poets* (1996). He released the rap CD, *25 Years* (1996), published *Branches of The Tree of Life:* The Collected *Poems of Abiodun Oyewole 1969-2013* (2014), is the editor of *Black Lives Have Always Mattered, A Collection of*

Essays, Poems, and Personal Narratives (2017), and *The Beauty of Being, A Collection of Fables, Short Stories & Essays* (2018). He released the song albums, *Gratitude* (2014), and *Love Has No Season* (2014).

Oyewole received his BS in biology and BA in communications at Shaw University, an MA in education at Columbia University, and is a Columbia Charles H. Revson Fellow (1989). Over the years, Oyewole has collaborated on more than a dozen albums and several books. He writes poetry almost every day, travels around the world performing poetry, teaches workshops, gives lectures on poetry, history and politics; and holds a weekly salon for artists, poets and writers in his home in Harlem, New York. ◉

ABOUT THE
CONTRIBUTOR

PHOTO: Suzy Gorman

LYAH BETH LEFLORE is a Bestselling Author, television and film producer, and music supervisor. As a thirty year entertainment veteran she has worked at Nickelodeon, Uptown Records/Entertainment, Wolf Films/Universal, and ran Alan Haymon Development for over a decade. LeFlore has also written eight critically-acclaimed books. Currently, she has several high profile tv projects in development including *Ferguson* with Undisputed Cinema/Touchstone TV; and *Things That Make White People Uncomfortable* with John Wells/HBO Max. She is the cofounder and executive director of the literary arts-based nonprofit,

The Shirley Bradley LeFlore Foundation/Creative Arts and Expression Laboratory, which honors LeFlore's late mother, St. Louis Poet Laureate Emeritus, and 2Leaf Press author, Shirley Bradley Price LeFlore.◙

OTHER BOOKS BY 2LEAF PRESS

2LEAF PRESS challenges the status quo by publishing alternative fiction, non-fiction, poetry and bilingual works by activists, academics, poets and authors dedicated to diversity and social justice with scholarship that is accessible to the general public. 2LEAF PRESS produces high quality and beautifully produced hardcover, paperback and ebook formats through our series: *2LP Explorations in Diversity, 2LP University Books, 2LP Classics, 2LP Translations, Nuyorican World Series,* and *2LP Current Affairs, Culture & Politics.* Below is a selection of 2LEAF PRESS' published titles.

2LP EXPLORATIONS IN DIVERSITY
Substance of Fire: Gender and Race in the College Classroom
by Claire Millikin
Foreword by R. Joseph Rodríguez, Afterword by Richard Delgado
Contributed material by Riley Blanks, Blake Calhoun, Rox Trujillo

Black Lives Have Always Mattered
A Collection of Essays, Poems, and Personal Narratives
Edited by Abiodun Oyewole

The Beiging of America:
Personal Narratives about Being Mixed Race in the 21st Century
Edited by Cathy J. Schlund-Vials, Sean Frederick Forbes, Tara Betts
with an Afterword by Heidi Durrow

What Does it Mean to be White in America?
Breaking the White Code of Silence, A Collection of Personal Narratives
Edited by Gabrielle David and Sean Frederick Forbes
Introduction by Debby Irving and Afterword by Tara Betts

2LP CLASSICS
Adventures in Black and White
Edited and with a critical introduction by Tara Betts
by Philippa Duke Schuyler

Monsters: Mary Shelley's Frankenstein and Mathilda
by Mary Shelley, edited by Claire Millikin Raymond

2LP TRANSLATIONS
Birds on the Kiswar Tree
by Odi Gonzales, Translated by Lynn Levin
Bilingual: English/Spanish

Incessant Beauty, A Bilingual Anthology
by Ana Rossetti, Edited and Translated by Carmela Ferradáns
Bilingual: English/Spanish

NUYORICAN WORLD SERIES
Our Nuyorican Thing, The Birth of a Self-Made Identity
by Samuel Carrion Diaz, with an Introduction by Urayoán Noel
Bilingual: English/Spanish

Hey Yo! Yo Soy!, 40 Years of Nuyorican Street Poetry,
The Collected Works of Jesús Papoleto Meléndez
Bilingual: English/Spanish

LITERARY NONFICTION
No Vacancy; Homeless Women in Paradise
by Michael Reid

The Beauty of Being, A Collection of Fables, Short Stories & Essays
by Abiodun Oyewole

WHEREABOUTS: Stepping Out of Place,
An Outside in Literary & Travel Magazine Anthology
Edited by Brandi Dawn Henderson

PLAYS
Rivers of Women, The Play
by Shirley Bradley LeFlore, with photographs by Michael J. Bracey

AUTOBIOGRAPHIES/MEMOIRS/BIOGRAPHIES
Trailblazers, Black Women Who Helped Make America Great
American Firsts/American Icons
by Gabrielle David

Mother of Orphans
The True and Curious Story of Irish Alice, A Colored Man's Widow
by Dedria Humphries Barker

Strength of Soul
by Naomi Raquel Enright

Dream of the Water Children:
Memory and Mourning in the Black Pacific
by Fredrick D. Kakinami Cloyd
Foreword by Velina Hasu Houston, Introduction by Gerald Horne
Edited by Karen Chau

The Fourth Moment: Journeys from the Known to the Unknown, A Memoir
by Carole J. Garrison, Introduction by Sarah Willis

POETRY
PAPOLíTICO, Poems of a Political Persuasion
by Jesús Papoleto Meléndez
with an Introduction by Joel Kovel and DeeDee Halleck

Critics of Mystery Marvel, Collected Poems
by Youssef Alaoui, with an Introduction by Laila Halaby

shrimp
by jason vasser-elong, with an Introduction by Michael Castro
The Revlon Slough, New and Selected Poems
by Ray DiZazzo, with an Introduction by Claire Millikin

A Country Without Borders: Poems and Stories of Kashmir
by Lalita Pandit Hogan, with an Introduction by Frederick Luis Aldama

Branches of the Tree of Life
The Collected Poems of Abiodun Oyewole 1969-2013
by Abiodun Oyewole, edited by Gabrielle David
with an Introduction by Betty J. Dopson

FLORIDA | NEW YORK
www.2leafpress.org